CON GRATU LATI ONS

YOU ARE

SRIMATHI KRISHNAN

notionpress.com

INDIA · SINGAPORE · MALAYSIA

Notion Press

Old No. 38, New No. 6
McNichols Road, Chetpet
Chennai - 600 031

First Published by Notion Press 2020
Copyright © Srimathi Krishnan 2020
All Rights Reserved.

ISBN 978-1-64828-837-1

Dedicated to my father & mother

Mr. P. Krishnan

&

K. Leela

CONTENTS

FOREWORD

I am delighted to congratulate Ms. Srimathi Krishnan for writing a text book on employability skills, which is the all-important text for students as well as job seekers. The intent of the author is to convince readers, i.e., students and job seekers to comprehend, that employability skills is not an innate quality. It can be acquired over a period of time, if a person is dedicated and committed towards oneself. The readers can be benefitted as to how to groom themselves for an interview, probable and frequent questions asked by HR personnel, how to overcome fear, ridicule and shyness and lot more. In general, this book will be benefitted for people who are fresh (out of college), one to five years experienced and for people who are experienced but still needs refinement in few areas.

This book presents the analysis done by various 'Data Mining' people and their findings about the ratio of graduates getting employed after their basic degree, the ratio of graduates getting employed in their specific domain and the skills they lack for getting employed.

Not only has the book highlighted about the setbacks which the graduates encounter but also the solution to overcome those challenges. It has stressed on the skills and the traits that is required for getting employed. The author has explained as to why interviews are nightmare for many? She has shared her professional experiences she had in her corporate journey. Each quotient has been explained in detail along with the author's experiences and with real time scenarios.

This book has also emphasized about the importance of effective communication skills with regard to time, language and cost-effectiveness and the four arms of communication viz, reading, listening, writing and speaking as well. As we say, grooming plays a vital role in a person's professional life, the author has also included grooming techniques as a part of the content for both the genders. Each and every aspect of grooming has been mentioned for easy reference.

In the later part of the book, the interview etiquette has been mentioned for the people who are in need of a job or people who are seeking a job and probable interview questions and probable answers for those questions. As a finishing touch, a few questions wherein the interviewee could ask the interviewer to understand that he/she is the person whom they are looking for "Bold ways to end an interview".

Eventually, the author has concluded the book with the attributes required to be successful in a job interview.

It is my hope and expectation that this book will provide an effective learning platform and reference resource for all job seekers, leading to an improved professional life.

Rajesh Raghupathi

SELP, Harvard Business School, Ph. D (Microbiology)
Bharathidasan University,

M Phil (Bio-Chemistry), MSc (Bio-Chemistry)
PSG College of Arts and Science,

PGDBA (Business), Symbiosis Institute, Pune

CEO, RND Softech Pvt Ltd

EMPLOYABILITY SKILLS

Employment – A positive arena to showcase your talent!

Employability cannot be explained in a single word; it's an ongoing and burgeoning topic. The significance of employability skills needs to be comprehended by one in order to be employed. In layman terms, employability skills can be defined as "a person or a candidate who possesses the required skills (good technical knowledge, great personal attributes, better understanding and subject knowledge) to get employed or to enter into one's aspiring dream job that matches one's qualification."

In line with the current trend, getting employed is not so hard, but getting a good job with a good salary, especially a job in one's domain, has become a hard nut to crack. According to a UN Labour report, unemployment in India is projected to witness a marginal increase between 2017 and 2018, indicating stagnation in job creation in the country. The United Nations International Labour Organization (ILO) released its *2017 World Employment and Social Outlook* report, which finds economic growth trends lagging behind employment needs and predicts both rising unemployment and worsening social inequality throughout 2017.

Job creation in India was not expected to pick up the pace in 2017 and 2018 as unemployment increased slightly, representing a near stagnation in percentage terms.

"Unemployment in India was projected to increase from 17.7 million last year to 17.8 million in 2017 and 18 million next year. In percentage terms, the unemployment rate will remain at 3.4 percent in 2017–18," the report added.

Our world has become highly competitive; in a broader view, the unemployment percentage may look lesser when we say 3%, 4% and so on, but that doesn't matter at all. When we comprehend that this 3% and 4% is out of many millions or even a billion (the current population of India is 1,358,137,719 as on Thursday, February 7th 2019. Based on the latest United Nations estimates, it is 1.35 billion), then it becomes a giant wheel. The percentage of unemployment becomes a herculean task to deal with. Dealing with the unemployment percentage at a macro level becomes an infinite task; instead, we need to deal with it from a micro or even a nano level, starting with each individual.

In such a scenario, every individual who is yearning for a job is a potential threat or say a potential competitor to another who is equally qualified. Getting the right job with a good salary is really hard. Now the question arises, *why is it a hard nut to crack?* Our country churns out millions of students holding a professional qualification in a year; for example, if we take the engineering domain, there are millions of students passing out as engineers every year.

In reality though, according to the Economic Times (2013–2014), the fact remains that 20–33% out of the 1.5 million engineering graduates passing out every year run the risk of not getting a job at all. Only 7% of engineering graduates are employable as identified in a 2016 survey done by an employment solutions company. They say, "As many as 97% of graduating engineers want jobs either in software engineering or core engineering. However, only 3% have suitable skills to be employed in the software or product market, and only 7% can handle core engineering tasks."

The major reason they quote: "Problems with the English language along with issues in computer programming make these students ineligible for employment. The difference in English and cognitive skill modules may only be a function of the input quality of the students. There is a consistent trend that the maximum gap is in computer programming, followed by cognitive skills and English and least in another domain's skills."

Let's analyse the current scenario. Are all students placed? If so, are they well placed in a good position in a corporate or in their qualified domain? Not really. Consider the example of mechanical engineering. Many students enter into the Information Technology (IT) field or into a BPO or KPO after completing their mechanical engineering. Some students are not even placed, and they keep hunting for a job even after their graduation.

This book is going to help those qualified students who are still in the pursuit of jobs even after their graduation but who fail to present themselves effectively when it comes to the interviewing process or group discussion.

Most of the time in job interviews, interviewers keep talking and grumbling about skills, skills, skills… (We don't think you have the required communication skills; you don't match our skill set, etc.) Yes, it's irritating to listen to it. Why are these corporate and job providers so specific about skills? And if you have a qualified degree, why do they keep questioning about skills?

Yes, that's the right question. Here it goes. When the interviewers mention about skills, it is not that they're commenting on you personally. They are mentioning general skills that are required for a person to get employed, irrespective of the domain you are in. There are a few skills that one needs to possess to get employed.

Skills required for getting employed

The skills and qualities mentioned below are general and not mentioned specific to any domain:

- Attractive resume
- Effective communication skills
- Grooming skills
- Good knowledge and content about your subject/domain
- Basic workplace etiquette viz., good body language
- Strong general knowledge

These are important attributes required for getting employed:

- Right attitude
- Passion
- Self-confidence
- Creativeness (out of the box thinker)
- Resilience
- High dedication and focus on goals
- Hard and smart work ethics
- Integrity

All these skills and qualities mentioned above are general and they vary from place to place according to the job requirement. But in general, if one possesses all these skills and qualities, there are very marginal chances of the candidate getting rejected by the interviewer.

Before sharing the knowledge of *how to acquire those skills and improve those qualities,* we will see **why interviews and group discussions are a nightmare for many people.**

Yes, for some people it is a nightmare. They panic and become anxious, and they feel that they are going to be humiliated in the interview. They downplay themselves thinking "I can't make it." The reasons for that could be:

➢ Lack of self-confidence

➢ Fear of failure

➢ Fear of ridicule

➢ Feeling shy to face people

Lack of self-confidence

How to gain self-confidence?

People who have succeeded in their lives have believed in themselves. It is not an innate quality for any person; over a period of time, they started acquiring self-confidence by way of practice and by believing in themselves. Self-confidence is not a stimulant which you purchase over the counter and once you consume it you feel confident about yourself. If that were the case, all people who feel very low about themselves would have purchased tonnes of stimulants to increase their confidence levels.

That's not how it's built; it's an attribute, which should come from within and when it does, you start believing in yourself. It needs to be practised, every minute, every second, to make it more comprehensible. Every time when you inhale and exhale, you should start believing and practising that "YES I CAN DO IT!" Continuous practice gives you a positive result. It is a magic mantra, and it works!

Whenever you feel very low, just rewind your life and think about happy moments; think of your good old days, starting from your school days. Remember that whenever you have thought, "No, it's not possible for me," eventually you have made it happen. For example, for someone, it could have been a nightmare to clear their board exams or to get distinction. But, ultimately, when you look at yourself, you would have made it happen. These are a few examples. Just think over it; you will have many incidents to quote in your life.

In my life, I would say participating in a debate or elocution or beauty contest was a nightmare. In the end, when I think of those days, I realise that I have done all those things successfully during my college days. Here I have mentioned "successfully," because I know there were many of my friends who had a wish at least to participate in those events. Yet having a wish in their mind, they couldn't make it happen because they were either scared of failure, lacked self-confidence, feared ridicule or they were feeling shy. Looking at them, I felt I was successful in participating in all those events and I even won a few competitions as well.

All those events were my stepping stones. Whenever I feel low, I think about those frozen moments and cherish them, and I gain confidence. I hope you all have such kind of incidents in your life to quote. Why don't you try doing the same? It really helps.

The first thing you should do to gain self-confidence is that you should STOP comparing yourself to others and you should not encourage people who compare you with others. God has made each and every person unique. And you are one of a kind. Nobody can compete with you because you are unique in your own way. The flair that you have in a particular domain will not be there with another person. It's high time;

awake and arise and start believing in yourself. If you don't believe in you, then no one else will believe you. "YOU CAN BELIEVE" in this mantra!

Fear of failure

The irony is every successful speaker (in their first speech) or a debater (in their first debate) or an HR person (in their first interview) would have faced this trouble – the fear of failure.

Then the question arises "how was it possible for them to make it happen?" All successful persons in their life had to cross this phase in their initial stages. Only those who had the valour to overcome those frightful moments of life became successful; the rest are the epitome of fright.

Failure is the stepping stone to success

It is a very famous quote, which all of you would have heard ample times in your life. But that is the truth of life as well; only a handful of people or hardly a few are exceptions. I will say failure is not at all a mistake; it becomes a real big mistake only when you do not learn anything out of it. If you have been rejected in one interview, or a second and third, don't worry. It's not a mistake. Only when you don't observe and analyse the reason for rejection, it becomes a real big mistake. You need to progress and rectify your errors in the next interview.

Every time you attend an interview, gauge yourself, whether you have rectified the mistakes that you have made the last time. This will help you increase your chance of getting selected in the forthcoming interviews.

Face anything and everything in life boldly. You cannot escape from anything in your life; you know that very well. Instead of facing it with a fear of failure, try facing it boldly. If you are mighty and optimistic, you will feel that things around you are very positive and all things are in your favour.

Think about your childhood days. Can you remember your childhood dreams about your future?

"…I want to be a pilot; only then I can soar high up until the sky. Soar high without any worries along with the birds, touch the mountain peaks, travel to strange, faraway places, stay in a fancy hotel and order different cuisines…"

I never had a fear that this might actually come true.

As children, our dreams never become spooky. As an adult, slowly our dreams vanish and become spooky because of the environment we live in. Just think about your childhood days; if you couldn't recollect, just observe a small kid. You can learn so many things from them – starting from three months old, the kid starts trying to fall upside down, then it tries to crawl pushing its hands and legs, then after that, it tries to hold an object as a support to stand and then it tries to walk.

In this cycle, if you observe very keenly, have you ever seen a kid falling upside down the very first time without any attempt? Have you heard or seen it anywhere? No, it never happens with any kid. The kid tries doing it ample times, and

at last, the kid succeeds. Can you say that when the kid tried falling upside down for the first time, it couldn't make it happen in the first attempt, so the kid has failed? Can you say that the kid will never try falling upside down again? Nope!

When you notice very keenly, you realise we were warriors when we were kids; we had the mind to fight against odds and the willpower to struggle without the fear of failure. We just made it happen. It's a fact. We all are walking now, so it's a true example that we were warriors and we didn't have any fear of failure in our childhood days. But what is stopping us now from doing it?

As we grew, we started feeling scared of our neighbours, society… everything became a phobia and we became sceptical in whatever we do. Day by day, we started letting go of our braveness… we wrap it up and fold it neatly and keep it inside a strong room, so that neither we will be able to break it open, nor can anyone steal it as well. That's when fear comes in and rules everyone. But some people keep continuing with their childhood braveness and they become successful.

It's high time to break-open your strong room and take back your braveness and weapons and become a warrior to face the battle with courage. Failure is your first success symbol; or you can call it a sign for your success. You need to keep continuing with your battle until you get to your destination – SUCCESS.

Fear of ridicule

As I mentioned in the earlier points, all great and famous personalities had this fear of ridicule as well. It's nothing new for you and me to face it alone. All successful persons had to cross this stage, yet only persons who had a positive mind to take all ridicule as a fuel to charge them up tasted success in their life. Just keep one thing in your mind: only people who are not in their normal senses will make fun out of others. People who are in their normal state will never make fun of others; rather they will be helpful for others growth or they will be silent, not hurting or disturbing others. They will not be a hurdle for others' growth.

When a person who is not in his senses is making fun of you, will it bother you in any way? Just think over it. If you are going to attend an interview, what is the maximum that can happen? Eventually, they can select you or they can reject you. Just think, if you are rejected, who is going to make fun of you? Even if there is someone to make fun of you, it's good.

Transfer that into positive energy and use that as your fuel to charge yourself up; don't get dejected at any time. Rise up like a power-packed jet and fly high with no fear; fly high with confidence, as no one can stop you – the sky is your limit.

I would like to quote my own story in this scenario. When I completed my under-graduation and post-graduation, I thought people would be in search of me. They would call me and offer me jobs and I would be confused about choosing which one would be the best fit for me. I was building castles in the air during my final year post-graduation.

After completing the course, I realised that there were many of my seniors who were still hunting for jobs after completing their post-graduation. The moment I heard that news, my castle started vanishing slowly. Then I realised the hardcore reality of life – that life is not as easy as I thought and it is never a cakewalk.

Then the usual story of any graduate started in my life as well. Only a few are blessed and fortunate to get a job immediately after their graduation or post-graduation. For me it was upside down; I had to hunt for jobs. I attended many job interviews, but I was not selected or it was not my cup of tea. But I was not dejected by any of the rejections; I had little worries, which I should genuinely agree. But every time when I got rejected, I kept telling myself **"SOMETHING BETTER IS AWAITING YOUR WAY."**

I charged up on my own; I was not waiting for someone to motivate me or raise me up. I stood up on my own whenever I fell down. I asked myself, "What is it that I need?" Yes, as every graduate aspires, I also had a wish to enter into the corporate world, but how? That was a thought-provoking question for me. Being an introvert, how could I get into the corporate world? There came a twist in my story.

As I mentioned earlier, the **'n'** number of interviews that I attended after my post-graduation and the events that I participated during my college days, viz., debates and elocution gave me the strength to make it happen. Because of all those endeavours and endurance, I sailed through. I got to know the ratio of blending qualities and skills in the right proportion to reach success.

Whenever I attended an interview, I used to evaluate and analyse what kind of mistakes I used to make often and what were the improvisations needed to be done. Having thought about that, I would gauge myself with the previous interview and see how far I had climbed up on the ladder. This is how I used to push myself to reach my goal.

After deciding to enter into the corporate world, I attended one more interview in a renowned corporate through an HR consultancy. They selected me, but I was not convinced because it was a sales job. I never wanted to enter into sales. Then somehow, I got convinced and joined the company in the sales department.

The initial three months were going well, and then I tasted a drop of a real sales job. That's when I felt I needed to move out of sales. Then, in the same company, I moved to a back-office position, and hence my journey and growth started in the corporate world. From there I started learning what life is all about and the thirst for learning made me improve my communication skills.

A person who was scared to talk to her friends in English and a person who did not have the guts to face people has become a trainer now, training corporate and college students. It's not a very hard nut to crack if you have the mind and confidence to face anything boldly.

A few tips to reduce nervousness immediately

If you are going to address a group of people, whether it is a speech or a job interview or a group discussion or whatever it may be, before entering into the hall, you can do this:

Move to a calm and peaceful place, and for two minutes, slowly inhale and then slowly exhale through your nostrils. Do this at least three times.

After completing that, the next exercise is to slowly inhale through your left nostril, closing your right nostril with your right-hand thumb finger, as shown in Fig 1(a), and exhale through your right nostril by letting go of the right nostril and closing your left nostril, as shown Fig 1(b) below for reference.

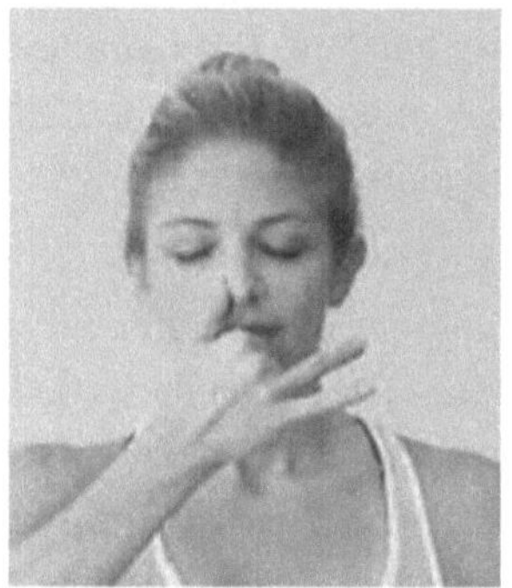

Fig 1(a)

Fig 1(b)

Then practice vice versa. Inhale through your right nostril by closing your left nostril as shown in Fig 1(b), and exhale through your left nostril by holding your right nostril as shown in Fig 1(a) for your reference. Do it the same way thrice. Just see the magic; your nervousness will get reduced to some extent immediately.

Feeling shy to face people

Why do people feel shy?

People feel shy only when they are asked to do something new or something that they have not experienced before. Most of the people feel shy to do things in front of a crowd or in front of other people. What do Abraham Lincoln, Albert Einstein, Thomas Edison, Brad Pitt, Tom Cruise and Jim Carrey all have in common? They were all victims of shyness in their childhood. But as these famous folks exhibited, it is possible to overcome shyness.

Shyness is defined as anxiety and behavioural inhibitions in social situations. One good example of shyness is to recollect your childhood days when some guests would have come home. Some kids immediately respond to the guest's questions such as "What is your name?" "Which standard are you studying in?" "In which school are you studying?"

But some kids never open their mouth. They always stand behind their mother and keep pulling their dupatta or saree to hide them. Some kids respond to their question when the guests step out of their home, but most of the kids never open their mouth until they step out. Even if the guests come twice or thrice, they never open up out of shyness. But when they come for the fourth or fifth time, then they slowly tell their name and the conversation starts. If the kids start feeling comfortable, then they show their naughtiness.

I hope all of us would have experienced this. In the same way, like a guest coming to your home, you need to attend interviews at least three to four times; then the fifth time you will start feeling comfortable and you will unwind your potential. This is how any introvert person becomes an ambivert or an extrovert.

Shyness is not a disease. It is something to deal with easily if we work on it on a daily basis. Overall, life is all about experiences. The experiences can be either bitter or sweet, yet we need to sail through it. Take each and every moment as a lesson and learn from it.

Change is the only constant thing that never changes in anyone's life.

No one can be a winner for a long time, and no one can be a loser for a long time. I would like to quote a few lines by Ms Kiran Bedi from a TED Women's speech she gave in December 2010 in Washington DC.

"I learned two essential things from my parents: Life is on an incline; either you go up, or you come down, it's your choice. And the second thing was, hundreds of things happen in your life, good or bad. Out of a hundred, ninety are your creations. If it is good, you enjoy it; if it is bad, all are your creations. You learn from it. The rest ten are nature set, over which you cannot do anything about it, you just got to respond to the situation. It's like a death of your relative or a cyclone or a hurricane or an earthquake. I truly believe this is the philosophy of life."

It's your turn to decide now whether you need to go up or come down in your life. The choice is in your hands. You are the best person to choose the best option for your life. All the best to choose the right answer.

SKILLS REQUIRED TO GET EMPLOYED

Attractive resume

Resume – in layman terms, it is a short document which carries a person's personal and professional data.

A resume is a one to two-page formal document that lists a job applicant's work experience, education and skills. A resume is designed to provide a detailed summary of an applicant's qualifications for a particular job.

A resume is the first document through which an HR person shortlists a candidate. The resume should be clear, precise, crisp and concise. Only an attractive resume will create a first good impression about the candidate. Here "attractive" doesn't mean a colourful resume. It is meant for the content in the resume. Every candidate should take ample time in preparing the resume.

I do understand that not all are good writers and everyone does not have experience in creating an attractive resume. If you do not have the skill to make your resume attractive, don't worry. If you are ready to spend some money, you can get good experts to write your resume.

Many job consultants and HR solution companies have come up with "resume writing services." These job consultants have appointed experienced resume writers and experts in this field. If you give your details to them, they will prepare at least three different styles of resumes according to your requirement. If this service is not affordable, you get so many sample formats when you surf the internet, and you could select one of your choice that suits you better.

I will just mention a few sample formats of resume for your reference that you can try to fit for your resume preparation.

Sample Resume for Graduate Students

Resume: One

Smrithi XXXXXX

Contact No:- 9XXXXXXX

Email Id:- sXXXXXXXX@yahoo.in

Career Objective

To work for a professionally managed company with good organisational objectives and a friendly environment in a capacity that offers responsibility, challenges, job satisfaction and scope for organisational and personal development and growth.

Academic Qualification

-B.Com Graduation XXXXXXX University

-Higher Secondary Certificate (H.S.C) XXXXXXXXX Board

-Secondary school Certificate (SSC) XXXXXXXX Board

Work Experience

Company - XXXXXXXX

Job title - Telecaller

Duration - XXXXXX

Responsibility

-Making outbound calls

-Handling customer queries

-Achieving targets

-Backend work

Company - XXXXXXXX

Job title - Business Coordinator

Duration - XXXXXX

Responsibility

-Making outbound calls

-Handling customer queries

-Achieving targets

-Backend work

-Handling petty cash

-Coordinating with other branches

Company - XXXXXXX

Job title - CSR

Duration - XXXXXX

Responsibility

-Handling inbound calls

-Admin work

Personal Skill Sets

-Ability to enable teamwork

-Strong willingness to learn new skills and abilities and observe perception

-Initiative for taking new responsibilities and high interpersonal skills

-Likes to interact with people to know, understand and help them solve their problems

-Good communication, analytical and interpersonal skills

Personal Details
Date of Birth: 5th July 1989
Language:
Address:

Sample Resume for an IT Graduate

Resume: Two

Anjhana ******

Email Id: anju.****@gmail.com

Mobile: 97*********

Summary of Technical Qualifications

-X years of experience as a java programmer -Experience in web-based Internet technologies which includes Java, J2EE Servlet, JSP, Java Beans, XML, HTML, JDBC and MVC

-Having knowledge in Struts

-A quick study with an ability to easily assimilate new ideas, concepts, methods and techniques

-Proven ability to analyse, design and code

-Dedicated, innovative, good co-ordination skills and self-motivated team member

-Good communication and team skills

Career Objective

To secure a challenging position where I can effectively contribute my skills as a software professional possessing competent technical skills.

Technical Knowledge

Languages: JAVA, JAVA EE, JSP, Servlets, Jquery, Struts

Scripting Languages: JavaScript

Markup Languages: HTML, XML

Server: Tomcat 6.0

-IDE: NetBeans IDE 6.0.1

Database: SQL Server 2005

Version Control Tools: Visual Source Safe 2005

Job Profile

Employer: XXXX Pvt Ltd. Designation: Java Programmer Role: Analyse, Design and Code Duration: Jan 20XX – till date

1) Client: XXXX

Duration: Feb 20XX – till date Project Name: ***** Software: Java, JSP, Servlet, JavaScript, Ajax, NetBeans IDE 6.9.1, JavaBeans, SQL Server 2008 WebServer: IBM WebSphere 7.0

Description:

XXXX our integrated patient tracking system provides physicians and clinicians with an integrated system to track patients and their records. Integration with hospital management systems, speciality sub-systems (Pathology, Radiology and Laboratory etc.), billing sun-systems and clinical image processing sub-systems are an integral requirement of any patient management system. XXXX uses all the industry standards like HIPAA, DICOM and HL7 etc. XXXX is a complete web-based electronic patient record (EPR) system that automates patient records and clinical workflow.

It saves time by giving clinicians instant access to patients' demographic information, active medical problems, complete medical history, detailed results, medications, allergies and other information vital for informed decision making.

XXXX Scheduling allows for scheduling of patients using manual and automatic scheduling functions. It also allows referring physicians to remotely schedule patients for visits and displays conflicts in scheduling. It can double book resources and display all available time slots for a specified date or date range. It enhances re-scheduling, cancellation and patient no-show. It has a flag for patient arrival. Dynamic graphical reports and views are generated as daily appointments, waitlists and cancellations.

Responsibility:

-Requirement gathering

-Responsible for design and coding

-Migration to development server

2) Client: XXXXX

Duration: March 20XX to May 20XX

Project Name: XXXX

Software: Java, JSP, Servlet, JavaScript, Jquery, Ajax, JavaBeans, NetBeans IDE 6.0.1, SQL Server 2008

WebServer: Tomcat 6.0

Description:

XXXX is a ***** tracking software for horse racing. It comprises four modules: Horse Registration, Show Registration, Person Registration and Administrator.

Racehorses like **** horses, Trocha, Trocha Y Galope, Trote Y Galope are registered in this module. All the minute details about the horses are recorded like their colour, DOB, pedigree details, siblings and so forth. In Show Registration, we register shows and events. Then the horses are registered for an event, assigned #'s and their placements are calculated in this module.

Shows and events are held at particular dates and times. This module helps in scheduling horses for these shows and modules. It allows for registration of personal details. The person can be an owner, breeder, rider and member. Payments can also be made for members alone. As administrator, we can create users and roles and give access to the user based on their role in the organisation.

Responsibility:

-Requirement gathering

-Responsible for design, code and test

-In development and code testing

-Migration to development server and creating new environment

Achievements:

-Awarded as the "Best Team Player Of XXXX"

Other Certification

-"Diploma in Java Technologies" from XXXX

Academic Chronicle

-B.E. CSE from University 1(20XX – 20XX)

-H.S.C from CBSE Board (20XX – 20XX)

-S.S.L.C from CBSE Board (20XX – 20XX)

Personal Details

Date of Birth: 3rd March 19XX Languages: Tamil, Malayalam, Hindi, English

---

Sample Resume for IT Graduate (For freshers)

Resume: Three

Varsha XXXXX

Mobile: 8xxxxxxx

Email: vxxxxxxxx@gmail.com

CAREER OBJECTIVE

To reach the top level of technology by sheer hard work and constant adaptation with changing times

PROFESSIONAL QUALIFICATION

B.Tech (ECE) XXXXXXX College of Computer Sciences, from XXXXXX University

ACADEMIC QUALIFICATIONS

-Intermediate XXXXX College XXXXX Board -High School XXXXX College XXXXX Board

TECHNICAL SKILLS

Operating System: MS Windows(XP,7), Microsoft office Languages: C

Core Skills: Electronics Devices and Circuits, Digital

electronics, Communication system, Microprocessor 8085

ACADEMIC PROJECT

Project name: XXXXXXXX

Team Size: 4

Software: KEIL VISION 3

Description

-It has the potential to dramatically improve various industrial and service applications through automatic detection, unique identification and control.

-It is expected to provide immense supply chain efficiencies, reduced labour costs and accurate real-time resource information.

-It uses wireless technology operating with the 50 kHz to 2.5 GHz frequency range.

-An RFID system consists of an RFID tag or transponder that contains data about the tagged item/object, an antenna, an RF and a transceiver to generate RF signals.

-It is used for collecting data, which it passes to a host system for processing.

-Keil Software is used to provide software development tools for 8051 based microcontrollers.

SEMINAR

-VLSI DESIGN and EDA TOOLS

WORKSHOP

-ROBOTICS -Venue - XYZ

SUMMER INTERNSHIP

-Have done a certificate course in PC technician Comp TIA A+ at NIIT INFOTECH PRIVET LIMITED

-Have done six weeks of vocational summer training successfully after 3rd year at BSNL, XYZ

-Have done training at NIIT INFOTECH PRIVATE LIMITED on C

ACHIEVEMENTS

-Participated in interschool athletics meets and won prizes

-Participated in a nationwide campaign to popularise physics – APPRECIATING PHYSICS IN EVERYDAY LIFE – and won first prize

-Actively participated in school cultural functions and attended National Children Science Congress at the state level

-Participation in science debate "A century of physics -achievement and challenges" at state level

-Member of The Bharat Scouts and Guides in school

-An active member of the student welfare club in college
-Member of the technical festival team and organised technical quiz in college fest

HOBBIES

-Yoga

-Interacting with people

-Listening to music

-Watching movies

PERSONAL PROFILE

Date of Birth:

Address:

Languages known:

MBA Fresher Sample Resume

Resume: Four

Sweta

Email ID- *****@gmail.com

Contact No.- +91-********

Career Objective

To seek challenging avenues where my knowledge and experience match the organisation's growth

Profile Summary

-A dynamic and multitalented professional with exceptional financial knowledge having an MBA degree

-Experience in all financial aspects and policies for business aspects

-Expert in the implication of new financial policy for new business development

-Proficient in identifying new resources of funds and also investing them for getting good revenue

-Excellent in the utilisation of all resources

Personality traits

-Strong leadership and motivational skills

-Ability to handle pressure

-Excellent communication skills, both written and verbal

-Ability to handle the team

Academia

-MBA in Finance with 81%

-B.COM in Commerce with 83%

-Intermediate from ASD college with 85%

-SSC from DSF College with 82%

Project

Name- Resource allocation of funds

Description- I was analysing resources of funds in ASD Company and for that, I have worked with the finance department

Computer Knowledge

-Proficient with MS office

-Internet savvy

Extra-Curricular Activities

-Working as a radio jockey for a local radio station

-Providing support to NGOs

-Actively participating in SAVE THE TIGER campaign

Personal Details

-Languages Known- Hindi, English, Tamil

-Address- BSKBSKB

Why should you hire me? (The answer given below is a creative answer. You can try different answers using your creativity)

> I wouldn't say I'm the best candidate for the position
> which you are hiring for. But I can assure you that I will
> be one among the best candidates you're searching for. I
> can give my best to relate to the company's expectations
> from me and maintain high levels of integrity and put
> forth my fullest efforts towards the contribution of the
> organisation's growth.

An important point to be mentioned while preparing your resume is that all details provided by you in the resume should be genuine. You should not give any fake details in your resume. It becomes very easy for an HR person to find out whether the information provided by you is fake or genuine. Be honest and don't ever think that you can fool around with your resume; if you try to do so, then you are going to make your life miserable. If they find out that the details in your resume are deceitful, then getting another job will really be a herculean task in your life. Being honest and candid will enhance your quality and maximise your chance of getting selected for a job, provided you have the qualification and potential.

For any interview, an attractive resume plays a vital role. This is the first and foremost important document for any job interview. Be careful and cautious before preparing your resume. The amount of time and energy you spend on preparing and making your resume more attractive gives you better returns. It's like "wise investment, better returns."

Here investment is not money, but it's your time and energy and the better return is getting a good job. So, think before you write. If you have mentioned any qualification or additional certification details on your resume, then make sure that while going for a job interview you carry all those documents along with you. When you prepare your resume, you need to give two references, one could be personal and one could be professional. When you give two references, always inform the concerned person about it and take prior permission from them to mention their name and contact details on your resume.

Effective communication skills

Communication is a vital part of everyday life; it can be explained as *conveying a message from one person to another person, or from one person to two or more persons sharing one's ideas, information, messages (formal or informal) or thoughts.*

Then what is effective communication?

It is also conveying a message from one person to another or more than one person. But here it's mentioned as "effective" which means it can be with regard to time, language and cost-effectiveness. Effective communication is when a person or group of persons are able to listen prudently and comprehend what the speaker communicated to them. Errors occur when the communicated message is not given in the way it was intended to. Consider the following examples.

With regard to time

Scenario 1

Timely messages are always appreciated and rewarded. In the absence of your placement officer, you're asked to accompany one of your senior professors to invite the HR personnel of a reputed company to come to your institution for a placement drive. But unfortunately, your professor cannot accompany you on that day, so you and two of your friends decided to go meet the HR person. The HR person whom you're going to meet is a very busy person and has no time to listen to stories. You're given fifteen minutes appointment time to discuss things. The meeting starts with a self-introduction and after that an introduction about your institution. Those introductions last for fifteen minutes, and the HR person has to rush for a meeting because the time given is over. He leaves for the meeting.

Was the discussion timely? Was the intended purpose of the meeting met? Nope!

Scenario 2

At the same time, a day before the meeting, you send a concise email to the HR, stating the list of persons coming for the meeting and the purpose behind the meeting with a brief introduction about the institution. On the day of the meeting, you start with a brief outline about the purpose of the meeting and a brief introduction about your institution, before getting into the details of the meeting. You clearly communicate what's needed to the HR and he leaves for his next meeting.

Moral: The need to value time and timely communication are always recognised and cherished.

With regard to language

Scenario 1

We will take the same scenario. The HR person you're going to meet doesn't know the regional language as he is from some other state. He knows to speak English fluently, whereas you and your friends are not well versed in English and unable to communicate the message which needs to communicated before the time gets over. The HR person isn't impressed by the way you all communicated in English, and straight away rejects the proposal.

Was it an effective communication with regard to language? No...

Scenario 2

English is a commonly spoken language across the globe. With the same scenario taken, you and your team members were able to communicate fluently in English to the HR person, and the meeting went on well. You were able to impress the HR person. Eventually, he agreed to visit your institution for the placement drive.

Is it not an effective communication with regard to language? Yes, it is.

With regard to cost-effectiveness

You need to deliver very important and urgent information about the placement campaign to your friend who didn't attend the meeting on that particular day. You have two choices to give the information to your friend: either inform over the telephone or you can travel to your friend's place located far away and inform your friend.

Which one will be a cost-effective communication? Obviously, it's the first option.

From the examples mentioned above, one could clearly understand that communicating effectively with someone should be timely, cost-effective and in the language which the listener can comprehend.

In this scenario, I have mentioned communication skill as an important skill for getting a job because if you don't answer the interviewer's question on time or your answer is not a timely answer your job will be at stake. Even if you don't know the required language to communicate to the interviewer then again it's of no use.

If you would like to enter into the corporate world, you need to have good communication skills in English. Nowadays,

English has become very important to enter into the corporate world. Many graduates and postgraduates feel that they are mentally handicapped because they don't know to speak English fluently.

Learning any foreign language is not a tough task. We just need to know the basic rules of the language and observation plays a vital role in speaking a language. When we talk about corporates, interviews, GDs etc., the effective communication mode that I talk about is *English.*

Unless and until you are able to communicate in English at least to some extent, you will not be able to cope with the demanding needs for any kind of employment in corporates.

According to a recent report authored by Dr. Abusaleh Sheriff of the Centre For Research And Debates In Development Policy, New Delhi, and Amit Sharma, research analyst with the National Council for Applied Economic Research [2], those who speak English fluently earn up to 34% more than those who don't speak the language, confirming the link between knowledge of the English language and income potential.

Communication skills can be divided into four parts:

1. Listening
2. Speaking
3. Reading
4. Writing

Listening

In a job interview or a group discussion, listening plays a vital role. When the interviewer is questioning you, it's mandatory that you should listen to them prudently. If you don't listen to them keenly, you will not be able to answer their questions appropriately. Most of the students, out of anxiety, will not be able to listen to what others say. It often happens with many folks. It may be due to lack of self-confidence as I mentioned earlier. None of that should rule you.

Train your brain and mind that both are going to listen to you and act according to your instructions. Practice listening one hour a day. Listen to audios or videos in English and repeatedly keep doing this. You can surf and get some material on the internet or from some bookshops for listening skills. Listen to comprehension, and after that, there will be some questions asked based out of that passage. Try to answer those questions with the help of the audio you listened to. Keep doing this every day.

Listening to different audios and videos in English will enhance your listening skills. You will evidently know the difference in a few days and become an effective listener. Whenever you get a chance to listen, you should do it passionately. It can be news or a debate or a speech in English. Try to listen to it and gauge yourself. All these efforts will definitely help you during your interviews and group discussions.

Speaking

On the one hand, speaking is inevitable in everyone's life whether you like it or not. Every day, when we wake up and until we go to bed, we keep talking to someone – may be friends, colleagues, professors, parents, siblings, neighbours and even strangers. The list goes on endlessly, but the topic and the language we talk may differ. Yet speaking is inevitable in all these scenarios.

On the other hand, when it comes to the formal way of speaking in English, and in particular if we are not comfortable with the language in which we are speaking, then comes the kink for many students. Even an extrovert person will also limit their speech when the language is uncomfortable for them. There lies the challenge.

We should not treat this as a common problem and just ignore it saying out of hundred people ninety have this problem and so I'm not the only person. We should treat this as an individual problem and focus on how to overcome this trouble. Off late, speaking in English has also become inevitable in the corporate world and so *prevention is better than cure.*

You know very well that after your graduation you will be placed in a corporate and you will have to communicate in English to your colleagues. It's better to practice speaking English from your college days rather than facing disgraceful situations in your life in the future. It's better to learn something which is inevitable out of interest, rather than learning it forcefully. There is a huge difference between learning forcefully and learning with interest. I hope you agree with me.

Only when you start liking something you will be able to learn new things and explore. Every day whether you like it or not, you fix up your mind that today I'm going to speak to my friends in English at least ten sentences. Let them tease or demotivate you; you just have in your mind that nothing can stop you from doing it. That's the kind of determination you should carry. Else you will be carried away by their de-motivations.

Similarly, like listening skills, you get materials for speaking skills as well by surfing the internet and visiting a few bookshops. You can watch English news channels and English movies or watch speeches by famous orators in English. Listen to their pronunciation carefully, the stresses, pauses and the accent they speak with. Most of us who have MTI (Mother Tongue Influence) when we speak English can correct all those errors by watching English speeches, channels and movies.

Once you listen to those speeches and news, try replicating the same speech and record it and gauge yourself. If you feel you're not satisfied, you keep doing it repeatedly until you become satisfied. Take help from others to gauge your improvement. Do it consistently every day at least for an hour. You will obviously find a huge difference in your speaking skills. Practice! Practice! Practice! Only then you can reach your target. Only hard work, perseverance and focus towards your goal will fetch success in your life. It's my **five P's, success equation.**

PRACTICE + PERFECTION + PRESPIRATION + PERSEVERANCE + PATIENCE = SUCCESS

If you **practice** those things you want to achieve in life with **perfection** and with hard work and **perspiration**, you can achieve it through your **perseverance** and **patience**. You will own success one day.

Reading

Reading is also an important task when it comes to communication skills. In job interviews, they ask the interviewees to take up written tests. In most of the written tests, in the verbal aptitude part, they have reading-linked tests. There will be a passage given, and one will have to read the passage and answer the questions given below the passage. The questions would be related to the passage, and you will have to answer all those questions based on the passage you read.

Why are these types of tests given in job interviews? They are testing a candidate whether one will be eligible to handle client queries or will be able to read, understand client queries and answer them accordingly. If you are unable to understand and answer to their message properly, then there will be a time loss, quality loss and there can be a chance of client loss as well...

Every day keep reading newspaper and magazines. Try to read some novels or some simple books or blogs on the internet and try to build your vocabulary as well. Every day, try to learn a new word and try to use it in your day-to-day conversation. Keep a separate notebook to improve your vocabulary. Take a new word every day and find out the meaning and keep writing it in your notebook. It will help you to increase the quality of your speech and will help you with your listening skills, reading skills, speaking skills as well as your writing skills.

Initially, try to speak, read, listen and write in simple English. Don't try to speak, listen, read or write using jargons or high-level English words. You will surely get demotivated thinking that English is a tough language to learn.

The threshold should be marginal when you start initially, and then gradually increase your levels. While you read an article or newspaper or any blog, try to read it aloud. Why should you need to read aloud? Because it will help you concentrate better and all the sentences you read will reach your mind. The habit of reading is really a good one to improve your language skills. Reading the newspaper and listening to the news every day will help you improve your knowledge and will be helpful at the time of group discussion. You will have more points to contribute to the discussion, and it will improve your fluency in English and reduce your grammatical errors as well.

Some people read books and novels as a hobby. You can also try doing it during your spare time. Try to utilise your college library, or you have libraries outside and online libraries as well. Try utilising all those facilities to hone your skills.

Writing

Writing skills are also equally important when compared to other skills. Writing is even more critical than speaking because while a person speaks one can use slangs like, gonna, wanna, kinda, etc. (when it is a casual or an informal conversation), which are not allowed or applicable in the case of writing.

Whilst writing an article, blog or official letter, one needs to be very careful over language and grammar because an official document or record will be created which can be referred in future as well. To begin with, firstly, one should start to write a rough draft, then take a break and read it after some time. Then certainly one will make some changes to it.

Secondly, create one more rough draft and take a break. Then after some time again read it and do the necessary rectifications. Once that is done there will be an outline of what one is going to write.

Thirdly, coherently organise it based on the requirements of the topic. Once it is organised, try and create a duplicate copy and start writing with the first subtopic and continue until you finish with your duplicate copy.

The next step to look into is that one needs to have an eye over one's language and grammar while writing. As mentioned earlier, one needs to read a lot of books, journals and newspapers to improve language skills. Learn the basics of grammar, which is quintessential to learning any language. Without a strong foundation in grammar, learning any language will be a nightmare.

When a person wants to document something, being meticulous is essential. Unless and until the person is not confident enough to write something without any grammatical errors, one should not publicise it. The reason is people can easily spot out the grammatical errors while compared to speaking.

Generally, while using tenses, one should be very careful. Those are the basics of any language. Even people who speak good English have doubts about using *has, have, had and be* forms of verbs (is, am, are, was, were, will be). So, it's very common to have confusions in using all these words, but one is left with no other option other than preparing oneself to set the basics right in English.

All that a person needs to improve is just to speak and write in simple English without any basic grammatical errors. If a person wants to improve in writing skills, practice basic grammar and start writing at least a page in a day and get it rectified with someone who is good in English or from a literary person or an agent. This is how one can improve writing skills.

But once you start liking the subject and once your basics are set, then you will never stop writing or speaking English because it becomes very interesting. When it comes to a debate or group discussion or a writing competition, you will be very much excited to do it rather than being anxious or nervous. Just imagine, when other people are nervous and stressed about something at the same time, you are much excited about the event – then how cool and easy life would be? Yes!

Just think about it; you decide whether you want to be nervous or you want to be relaxed. If you are from a vernacular medium, initially learning on your own would be a little tough. So, you can join some spoken English classes which are good and worthwhile in your locality and start learning the basics. Ask questions and questions until you understand.

Don't ever feel that if you ask questions people will think of you as an ignorant person. No, never have that in your mind. Because you don't know English, that's the reason you have enrolled yourself in this class. If you don't ask questions or you don't clarify your doubts, it is a loss for you. Let people think whatever they feel like, but you keep asking questions and clarify your doubts.

Even after your class is over, spend one hour in a day to do some activities or tasks which will help you improve your English. As mentioned earlier, listen to some audios and news channels and read the newspaper. If you have any doubts about that note down in your notepad and next day clarify those doubts in your class. After your English classes are over don't stop learning English.

Learning is a continuous process and if you do it regularly, you will surely be more confident than before to learn on your own. Start doing things on your own without depending on others. If you have any doubts you can take help from your English professor or trainer in your college or any of your friends who are good in English.

Grooming Skills

Grooming means dressing well and caring about one's appearance and attire to make one presentable and appealing in front of others.

Research says that it will take six seconds or less to judge a person and decide whether he or she will be a good fit for the organisation by seeing their attire and appearance even before they speak. This statement explains how important grooming is when it comes to a job interview, although nothing takes the place of talent, hard work, knowledge and imbibed ability. Being well-groomed helps to be professionally, personally and socially appreciated.

Most people believe in the myth that grooming is something wrong and it pertains only to a certain profession. People think that only people who look good and resplendent can groom themselves and only for them it suits. It's totally a wrong statement. Everyone can maintain and groom themselves according to their facial structures and appearance, but the significant thing everyone should have in mind is that one should always groom themselves in the way which suits them better; else one will look unpleasant.

Every individual is unique and beautiful in their own way. You needn't compare yourself with any other person because you're unique. Most people think that grooming is a costly affair and everyone needs to go to a beauty salon to enrich their beauty. Grooming can be done by yourself without going to a beauty salon.

Grooming has become inevitable these days. Right from your attire, your hairdo and your skin, everything will be noticed by others, so carrying yourself in an enhanced way has become mandatory. You may wonder what grooming has to do with regard to getting a job.

What is the relationship between grooming and getting a job?

Grooming plays a vital role in shortlisting and hiring a candidate. For example, consider that you are an IT graduate and you have applied for a 'Client Relationship Executive' position in XYZ Company. For the same position from the same college, one more candidate with the same qualification has applied for that job. Both of you look good, appearance wise. The only difference between you and the other candidate is that the other candidate seems to be dressed well and looks very professional in all means. Apart from that, your technical knowledge, communication skills, confidence level and general knowledge are at par with the other person. But if at all there is a comparison between you and the other candidate, the only highlight is that the other candidate's grooming looks much better than yours. Rest all other qualities are the same. Whom do you think the company will prefer first?

I wouldn't say that grooming is the only essential criteria to get a job… nope. My point is, if the interviewers are meticulous, they'll even notice the way you groom and carry yourselves. If that is the case, I do not want any candidate to lose their job for even a small error. "Small drops make an ocean." Grooming also enhances your chance of getting selected. Rather than the interviewers being meticulous in all means, I want the job seekers to be more meticulous than the interviewers because you're the needy.

I presume that you would agree with my point. Grooming also plays a vital role in job interviews. Now, the question arises "How to self-groom without any flaws?"

When you attend an interview, things which you should pay more attention to are the following ones:

Hair

For women

Hair maintenance should be done properly. When it comes to hairdos, you should neatly do a hairdo which suits your face well and don't ever try a new hairstyle when you are going for an interview. An appropriate hairstyle gives structure to one's personality. If one chooses a wrong hairstyle or is unaware of what suits best with one's personality, one can never present themselves in the right manner.

If you don't feel comfortable, then that will become a hassle for you while attending the interview. Your hairdo should look formal and not casual. If you've done fringes, please do pin it up neatly so that you don't keep fiddling with your hair. If you do so, that may distract the interviewer or the other person in front of you.

Do not apply oil on your hair on that particular day. If you're so particular about oil, you can use hair gels or serum available in the market, which will not give a drab look on your face. If you apply oil on your scalp, after one or two hours, your face will look oily and ruin your appearance.

Don't use clips or bands which look gaudy or shiny. Use formal clips or bands, black or brown with no shiny stones on it.

If you colour your hair, the choice of your hair colour should be based on your skin texture and colour.

Nevertheless, HR personnel never like snappy colours in a formal interview platform because that will exhibit a casual and "don't care" impression about you. Hair maintenance plays a vital role, which means your hair should not be unkempt; it should be dandruff, lice and nits free. Otherwise your scalp will be itchy, and if it is seen obviously on your hair it will give an awkward look.

Hair length or style should be based on the kind of body structure one possesses and the profession one is in.

Body structure	Length
Heavy/short	Razor cut (Shoulder level)
Tall/heavy	Straight (long hair)
Underweight/skinny	Shoulder level/steps
Average height/shapely	Any hairstyle

To enrich your professional look (hair clips for your reference)

For men

Similar to girls, boys also should maintain their hair well. Your hairstyle should suit your face. Do a proper haircut before attending job interviews. Don't try a new haircut or style a day before your interview; if that doesn't suit you, your face will look awkward.

Mostly college going boys have weird hairstyles which are highly intolerable when it comes to job interviews. That illustrates your immaturity and the level of importance you exhibit for your job interview. It's always better to have a charming, good-looking and formal hairstyle and haircut while you attend an interview.

Do not use oil on your scalp on that particular day, as I told earlier for girls. The reason is the same. Instead, you can use hair gels or serums, which are available in all stores.

Hair colouring is not an important aspect. Despite that, if you're in need to colour your hair, you can use black shade to colour your hair. That is never a problem. But when you want to go for fashion colours and global colouring for interviews, it's highly not acceptable.

Spikes are also not acceptable; go for a formal haircut and good-looking hairstyle without any colours.

All these grooming procedures are not only applicable for freshers; they are applicable even for experienced persons as well, while gearing up in the ladder from one job to another. For every individual who is working for a corporate or any office grooming is mandatory.

Here I would like to quote a real-time example of a person who worked with me. His name is Jitesh. When he joined our company, he had close to two years of work experience. He was from a rural background and he got into our company as a sales officer and he was working with us for three years. He was always a topper and whenever I try to recall his face I remember him with a cap on his head. The reason was at the age of 24 he had become bald. He never removed his cap anytime, even during client visits or for any important meetings. But he had felt bad about it many a time.

That made him feel very embarrassed. At a particular incident, when he got a good offer from a leading bank as a 'Relationship Manager' to handle "high net worth clients" with a handsome salary and he had to meet the regional director of the bank for further rounds of interview, the Regional Director (RD) selected him seeing all his records, achievements, performance and his positive referral check. After the interview though, RD wanted to meet him again to ask him a question. He asked, "Everything I found in you is too good, but my only worry is your appearance."

Since the RD was a good person, he told him that the customers he was going to handle would be affluent and high net worth customers. Wearing a cap while meeting high net worth clients would not give a positive outlook. Immediately Jitesh questioned the RD, "Sir, what can I do for this? At the age of 24 I had extreme hair fall and from then I became bald. To hide that I'm wearing a cap."

Then the RD replied, "It's absolutely fine, but that doesn't give a good look on you. If it is a lower level position that I'm offering you, then it's fine. You're going to handle high net worth clients so everything counts. My advice to you is, go to a hair implant centre, take your own time, perhaps three to four months, implant new hair and come back. We will wait for you."

Since Jitesh met a good person, he got a chance to enhance his look and got a wonderful career. He did so as advised by the RD and did his hair implant. Now he is in a good position with the same bank and, as usual, is continuing as a performer in the bank. The reason to quote this example is that even for an experienced person with almost 6 years' experience as a top performer, grooming plays a vital role. No matter if you are a fresher or an experienced person, grooming is quintessential.

Ears and neck

For women

You can wear simple pearl studs or earrings to make you look more professional. Pearls are globally accepted professional wear; even you can wear a pearl chain on your neck that will also enhance your professional look. (Look at the below images for reference) Multiple piercings in your ears and wearing more than three or four earrings doesn't give a professional look. Better to remove all those earrings and wear one simple pearl stud which will give you a pristine professional look and with a pearl chain on your neck.

Earrings these types are allowed:

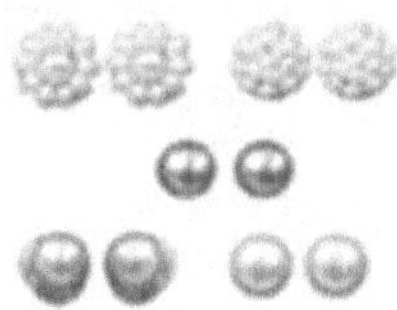

These are not allowed:

These types of neck sets are allowed:

These are not allowed:

Finger rings: Keep them simple and not chunky

Bracelets or bangles: You may wear either a bracelet or a bangle

These types of bracelets or bangles are allowed:

Avoid chunky bracelets or too many bangles

Face

For women

Don't overdo makeup and spoil your face. Mild makeup will always enhance your beauty.

If you're very specific about using eyeliner and mascara, use only a black shade. And using a foundation or any other cream should be used mildly. Use a subtle colour lipstick which is not seen obviously. Don't use lip gloss, which will distract others. Using blush, compact can be avoided. If required, everything can be used subtly.

And all these depend on your profession as well. If you have the practice of tweezing your eyebrows, do it a day before your interview and have a neat look. Keep a small black or plain maroon bindhi on your forehead and don't use bindhis with stones or designer ones.

To maintain your skin, you can do facial once in a month in a salon, or if you feel it is not affordable, you can always make yourself feel good by using most of the ingredients available in your kitchen.

For men

Hair on your face mostly should be avoided or else can be neatly trimmed. Preferably a clean shave is advisable and using of any creams can be done mildly. Wearing a neck chain and ear piercing are highly unacceptable when it comes to professional look.

If you would like to maintain your skin, a day or two days before your interview, you can do a facial from a salon. If it is not affordable, you can do a natural facial in your home by using natural ingredients. Not only by doing an outward cleansing you will look good, but your intake also should be nutritious and healthy; only then you will look active, energetic and glowing.

Common tips on skin maintenance

Did you know that skin is the biggest organ?

- Use only branded products for your skin or home remedies.
- Consume at least 12–14 glasses of water to keep your skin glowing and avoid oily food.
- Clean your skin with raw milk every morning/to remove makeup.
- Avoid dandruff as it leads to pimples/acne.
- Regular use of natural fruit packs will keep your skin young and wrinkle-free.

➤ Exfoliate your skin at least once a week to rejuvenate dead cells.

➤ Healthy skin reflects good health.

Hands and feet

For women

Hands and feet should be maintained hygienically. You can also do a pedicure and manicure to maintain your hands and feet. *Pedi* means *feet* and *cure* means *care*. Taking care of your feet is called pedicure. *Mani* means *hands* and *cure* means *care*. Maintaining your hands and fingers is called manicure. It is not mandatory that you will have to go to salons to do pedicure and manicure. You can do it in your home by using natural ingredients.

You should always maintain your hands and feet well. Cut your nails periodically and file them. If you want to use a nail polish, use only light colours, which will not distract others. Using dark colours like blue, yellow, orange, red or maroon is not advisable. You can use baby pink or transparent colours which will not distract others.

Don't grow your nails very long like a vampire or witch; cut it short and maintain a size which will look decent on your hands and feet. If you have very thick and bushy hair on your hand, if you feel uncomfortable about it, you can go for a waxing which will look good.

Tattoos and mehendi are to be removed or covered appropriately. Wearing anklets on your feet is not advisable. If you're very specific about it, wear a simple one, without bells in it. When you're choosing slippers/sandals or shoes for your official wear, go for simple plain black or brown shoes or slippers. Heels can be maximum ½ inch, and it should not make any noise while you walk.

Do not wear watches with stones or abnormally big ones that don't suit your hand. Some people out of belief would have tied some holy threads on their hands in different colours. If you feel that you can remove the threads for a day, it's good; else if you're so specific and you have a profound belief that removing the thread is not good, then no problem. You can go ahead with that.

Tips for women to take care of their hands and feet

Hands speak about how you lead life. Feet are the most abused and least cared for.

➢ Regular pedicure and manicure are mandatory
➢ Chipped nails/cracked skin reflect negatively on your personality
➢ Shape up your nails and keep them well painted or clean
➢ Use oil-based moisturisers to massage your hands and feet at bedtime to avoid wrinkles

Footwear

For women

Shoes with 1 ½ inch heels are standard. You may wear a pair with smaller heels or a flat pair. Stick with a black/brown pair. Be sure your shoes are polished and that your heels are intact.

➢ Do not wear colourful sandals
➢ Avoid heels and sandals with bling
➢ Avoid white coloured sandals as they get dirty easily. If you do wear them, clean them well.

For men

As I mentioned earlier for girls, you also should maintain your hands and feet hygienically. Otherwise, you'll be prone to get infections like fungus and formation of cracks on your heels, which may lead to severe pain and require medical attention. To avoid these kinds of hazards, maintaining your hands and feet in a proper hygienic way will be better always. *Prevention is better than cure.*

Do not wear any kind of weird bracelets. If you're very specific about valuable ornaments, you can wear a simple one. But, it is highly unadvisable. Wear a branded formal watch, which suits your hand, and do not wear a sports watch or a big dial that will give a casual look. Be always quality conscious.

Some people would have tied some holy threads on their hand. If you are so convinced that removing the thread will cause something bad, then you can tie it or it is advisable to remove it.

The shoes which you are going to wear should be formal ones. It can be black or brown, cut shoes or ones with laces; socks should be cleaned and washed every day and it should not stink. You can wear dark blue, black or dark grey socks. As a thumb rule, don't wear white socks.

When you are wearing the same pair of shoes every day, polish it well with a brush and use a shoe shiner to make it look shinier. Make sure your socks should be long enough not to expose your skin when you sit.

Attire

For women

When it comes to Indian outfits, you can go for a nice simple cotton salwar with light colours and which will not give you a dull look. Don't go for dark, chunky and gaudy dresses. When it comes to corporates, wearing a saree for an interview is not much advisable. If you're very specific about wearing a saree, you can go for plain simple cotton sarees.

The dress which you wear should give a formal look and should make you feel comfortable. If you wear a dress with which you are not feeling comfortable, that will ruin your interview. So, be very specific about your dressing.

If you want to go for western attire, go for a formal shirt and trousers. Your dress should be neatly pressed and tidy. When you wear western attire, you should go for shoes and not slippers. Use a roll-on deodorant or spray or a mild perfume to avoid your body odour. At the same time, you are not supposed to use a very strong perfume, which will distract others and it'll draw undue attention of others. You can test it choosing using testers and then purchase it.

There is something called as "power dressing," which means dressing in a way and style which gives you an authoritative and professional look. Power dressing is especially meant for professionals. The way you groom yourselves will enhance your look, and it will add or command respect to you. By seeing your dressing, people can decide whether you're a true professional or not. Always try to be a true professional when you are at work or if you are trying to get a job. It will enhance your look and increase your chance of getting selected.

For men

Formal attire can give you a truly professional look. Your clothes can make people remember your face. Your clothing should make you look good, not draw undue attention. We each have our own unique colouring, bone structure and facial shape. When you choose clothing that works with your individual characteristics, you look great. When you wear clothing that does not enhance your body structure or colouring, you appear sloppy or less attractive.

Clothing that doesn't suit you will be distracting to others. They will notice your accessories rather than your face. Choose fabrics, colours and styles that emphasise your good features and detract from your weaker features or figure flaws. You can go by brands for your formal attire, which will enhance your look and you can command respect. Go for lighter shades with mild prints, vertical stripes or plain shirts, either full-sleeved or half-sleeved. Go for colours like, beige, white, off-white, etc. You can even wear pale blue shirts.

Trousers should be dark preferably and you can go for colours like black, navy blue, brown, beige, etc. Note that the tie which you wear should complement your shirt colour. It is important to button up your shirt till the collar button. Black and navy blue are universally accepted colours for men.

Though you may wear beige trousers with a dark coloured shirt, try to have at least one pair of black trousers. Trousers may not have pleats. When you're wearing a belt, wear only formal belts with a sleek buckle. As a thumb rule, match your belt with your shoes.

Remember, trousers may or may not have pleats.

Just a quick check can help you enhance your look.

There is a saying "elephants don't bite but, mosquitoes do." Often the small things cause the bigger problems. When we have threads hanging off a well-stitched suit or buttons missing from a shirt, they will take away from your professional image.

As a rule, the simpler, the better.

Colours do convey

Colours and their meaning

- **White – tranquillity and peace**
- **Black – mystery/formal**
- **Navy blue/royal blue – openness of mind**

- **Red – sensuality**
- **Orange – passion/achiever**
- **Yellow – friendly**
- **Green – natural**
- **Brown – practicality**
- **Pink – innocence**
- **Grey – indecisive**

Black and navy blue are universally accepted colours for men

Socks

Choose a colour that coordinates with your trousers (usually black, dark grey, dark brown or dark blue).

Make sure they are long enough not to expose your skin when you sit.

As a thumb rule, do not wear white socks.

Wear clean socks; change them every day. You can dry the same in sunlight to avoid bad odour

Shoes

Wear a good pair of leather shoes – black, brown or tan shoes. Shoes must be polished every day.

Do not wear shoes that look casual or have worn out heels.

Belts

Wear only formal belts with a sleek buckle. As a thumb rule, match your belt to your shoes.

This type of buckle is acceptable

Avoid this type of buckle

Quick grooming checklist before you step out of your home

- ➢ Ensure hair is clean, well-combed and free of dandruff.
- ➢ Check that teeth are clean and no food is stuck in between your teeth. If your breath is not fresh, use a mouth fresher or just munch a few cardamom to get fresh breath.
- ➢ Ensure fingernails are clean and shaped with no chipped nail polish.
- ➢ No innerwear should be shown out.
- ➢ Shoes should be polished not worn down at the heel.

Grooming repairs should not be done in public. If you have to file a broken nail or pick spinach, mustard from your teeth, go to the nearest restroom.

Good knowledge and content about your subject

For example, if you are a mechanical engineering student and you are attending an interview with any of the automobile companies, ensure you are well dressed. You should have good communication skills and your resume should look very attractive.

Will all this lead you to get a job without having sound technical knowledge in your domain? Obviously not! If you aren't able to get through in your technical round and rest all other things fail. So, preparing for the technical round is equally important as other skills; surf on the internet and collect details about last year's technical questions and prepare well. Clarify your doubts with your professor. Try to be a little creative and innovative. This will leave a long-lasting impression on you.

Update yourself in your domain by looking into the latest automobile magazines and know about the latest technological advancements in your particular domain, may it be IT or CSE, mechanical, civil or aeronautical. If it is arts and science, surf for the latest management tools and have knowledge about the latest accounting software, etc. If you possess all the skills I have mentioned and with that if you are very strong and sound in your technical aspect as well, I'm telling you no one can stop you from getting a job.

Display your confidence and make them feel by your actions that their company will be benefitted and they will be proud if they appoint you as an employee. If you do not know answers to any of the questions they ask, please don't try to bluff. People in front of you are not fools; they can easily make out that you are trying to fool around, so don't ever do that.

Instead, you can frankly tell them that you do not know the answer, but surely you will update your knowledge and improve yourself. It is not mandatory that everyone should know the answer to all questions. Make yourself strong in basics and know the advancements in your field. The rest is destiny; don't feel too strongly for it. If it is destined for you, it will reach you at any cost. As I have mentioned earlier the five Ps equation. Follow this success mantra and the rest is destiny.

As a thumb rule *be honest*. Honesty is the best policy. To improve your knowledge in your domain, read lots of books and magazines about your area. Try to share it with your friends so that you can get in-depth knowledge. Try to discuss with your professors also; they can suggest you with better books or websites. Technical knowledge in your domain will help you increase your chance of getting selected.

Good general knowledge (GK)

In general, if a person has good IQ, that person will be considered as a matured and knowledgeable person. Strong general knowledge will help candidates in group discussions and interviews. If there is any written test round in interviews, HR will give you a general topic and ask you to write. If you have good general knowledge, it will help you to come up with points. Generally people like and appreciate persons with good general knowledge.

To improve your GK, you can read the newspaper and listen to news channels; you can update yourself with GK books. Whenever you get time, read a lot of books that will enhance your GK. This will help you improve your communication skills as well. A better way to improve your GK is to watch quizzes on television and listen and observe older people when they discuss socio-economic activities or about finance or anything about common topics.

ETIQUETTE

Etiquette can be defined as a set of basic behaviours or practices to be followed in a specific forum or wide variety of situations. Here I am going to mention about interview etiquette.

Interview etiquette

Any level of interview has a few common protocols to be followed; here are a few points to be followed before and during the interview.

Two days before the interview

➤ Take a sufficient number of copies of your resume.

➤ Select your attire and wear it and check for the fit and for any flaws in it.

➤ Create an interview checklist.

➤ Neatly press and keep your attire in the cupboard.

➤ Purchase a good-looking formal file to keep your resume and documents.

➤ Don't use a cover to keep your resume or don't fold your resume.

➤ Keep ready all your relevant documents and education credentials.

➤ Men can do your hair cut two days/a week before the interview.

➢ Keep your passport size photographs ready and have a soft copy of your passport size photograph as well.

A day before the interview

➢ If you're going to travel in your own vehicle, fill fuel a day before and check for any other flaws.

➢ Verify in your interview checklist whether all the points in the checklist are done If done, put a tick mark against that, else mark an "x" against that point.

On the day of the interview

➢ Start early from home and be there at the interview venue one hour before the specified time.

➢ Please avoid taking public transport on that particular day; take your parents, friends or relative's help to drop you there.

➢ Carry all the relevant documents required.

➢ Be calm and quiet.

➢ After reaching the venue, immediately switch off your mobile phone or put it in silent mode.

➢ During the waiting time don't keep messaging or talking to your friends over the phone.

➢ Wait for your turn; don't be in a hurry and keep on questioning about your turn.

➢ As mentioned earlier, during the time you're waiting, keep practising the exercises to reduce your nervousness.

➢ When your turn comes don't be nervous; stay calm and walk towards the interviewer cabin, knock the door mildly twice and then open the door slowly and ask, "Excuse me, sir/ma'am, may I come in?" When they say yes, then get in.

➤ While closing the door, close it mildly; don't bang the door. Open and close the door mildly when you enter and exit the cabin.

➤ You're not supposed to sit until you're asked to do so.

➤ As soon as you enter the cabin, wish the interview panel a good morning/afternoon with a warm and broad smile. If there is more than one female interviewer, then use ma'ams; more than one male, then use sirs.

➤ Don't be confused where to keep your file; if they ask a copy of your resume, open your file and give them a copy and place your file towards your right or left-hand side on the table or place it on your lap.

➤ Be confident and candid.

➤ Be crisp and don't drag your responses for the questions they ask you.

➤ Look into the interviewer's eyes and answer all the questions boldly with a sweet smile, but don't be overconfident or too smart.

➤ For any interview, the common questions would be:

- Tell me about yourself.
- Tell me about your strengths and weaknesses.
- Why did you choose this course?
- Why did you choose our company?
- What are your hobbies?
- What is your goal?

All these are general questions to check your communication skills, your creativity and your presence of mind. Try to answer all these questions in a different creative way, not in the usual style. But do not bluff. As I mentioned earlier, don't bluff but be honest and candid.

I would like to share some weird, real-time interview questions asked by a few corporates

1. If you were shrunk to the size of a pencil and put in a blender, how would you get out?

2. Rate yourself on a scale of 1 to 10 on how weird you are.

3. How many traffic lights are there in your city?

4. What do wood and alcohol have in common?

5. Why are manhole covers round?

6. Design an evacuation plan for your city.

7. How much should you charge to wash all the windows in your city?

Now you try to answer all these questions creatively; the answer should be creative, logical, meaningful and sensible. You can find answers to all these questions at the end of the book. But be honest; first, try to answer all these questions and then look at the end of the book for answers. The answers given at the end of the book are not the only apt and right answers; you can always try it differently on your own. These answers are creative.

I have given a possible answer, of course. I can't guarantee that the given answers will help you in getting the job, but at least you will be able to attend the interview confidently and you won't be wondering if such questions are really being asked in interviews. Yes, these questions are real-time interview questions and the major questions are asked by Google for its different positions. So, just pull your socks and join the creative question race and start triggering your brain with unexpected questions. Train your brain and make your interviewer smile broadly at you.

Answers to the interview questions

1. A. I would multiply into two try to get out of the blender.

    B. I would yell at the top of my voice for someone to save me before the blender is turned on.

2. A. It depends on the day. Yesterday I was an 8; today I'm down to a 2. It also depends on what standard of "normality" I'm comparing myself against.

    B. Fire is the only right answer. A truly weird person would answer with something completely unexpected. If I say 10, then I would come across as trying too hard to be weird. But if I say 1, then I would be trying too hard to be normal. No one is completely normal; everyone is slightly weird.

3. To be very honest, I have no clue about it. But for sure when I come here to collect my offer letter, I will let you know the exact numbers.

    A. I don't like estimating; I like concrete answers. I'd have to do some research to find out the true number of similarities between wood and alcohol.

    B. My bed frame is made of wood; both help me sleep.

    C. Both contain grain. I like both, so I'm not against the given in either case.

    Girls/boys who're not interested in answering this question can just reply, "Sorry, I'm not the apt person to answer this question, because I have not tasted alcohol in my lifetime. I'm a teetotaller, so I can't make out the common factor between wood and alcohol."

5. A. Because, they've always made them that way. Habits are hard to break.

6. A. To be very honest I didn't expect such a question today. And moreover, I'm not a civil engineer too. But, certainly if given a few days I would try making the plan.

7. A. As much as the market is willing to pay for.

   B. As much as I need to charge in order to hire all the homeless people in the city to do all the work, but where I would still make enough to be able to finance a startup for solving the unreasonable requests of the local government.

BOLD WAYS TO END AN INTERVIEW

1. Do I have this job?
2. Is there anything we discussed today that makes you feel that I am not the one for the job?
3. What can I do to convince you I'm the one for the job?

Attributes required for being successful in a job interview

Attitude

Carrying a positive attitude in all situations is mandatory. A positive attitude can impact each and every aspect of one's life. People who maintain a positive approach towards one's life in any kind of situations and challenges will be able to move forward more constructively than those who're stuck with a negative attitude.

Passion

Passion is the driving force in one's life. Passion is the positive affinity towards something. When you are passionate about something in your life, you will surely achieve it. Similarly, when you want to join your dream company, you should be yearning to achieve it. If you look at successful personalities, they all have a passion for whatever they do.

Success doesn't come as easily as you think. During the interview, the interviewers can feel the passion you've within for joining the company.

Creativity

Being creative is also an important attribute to get employed. "Think what others don't think and do what others don't do." Be unique in the crowd. Wherever you are, your work will be recognised and appreciated. All companies look for people who are creative and unique in their thoughts. Good creators are always innovative. They are always in the pursuit of new things, new ideas and new thoughts. They always feel fresh, energetic and vibrant. Being creative makes you feel positive, and the quest for knowledge never stops. You keep exploring new arenas.

Be creative in everything you do and reach greater heights. Even in interviews, they ask questions which you would never expect, but if you are creative, then you will be able to handle the situation well and think in a different perspective to answer the question.

Resilience

Even if your day is disastrous, you should be in a situation to bounce back and handle the situation. This is an essential attribute even in your personal life. If you are not able to overcome a bad day or an unexpected thing in your life, it means you are a coward and you try to escape from tough situations. Always try to erase unsolicited happenings in your life; this will help you to have a resilient nature and make you bounce back to your normal state.

Overall, be confident, well-groomed and well-prepared. Give it your best and always remain positive.